"What Do We Want?"

"FREEDOM!"

"When Do We Want It?"

"NOW!"

—Rallying call during civil rights marches

Courage in the Moment

THE CIVIL RIGHTS STRUGGLE, 1961-1964

Photographs by Jim Wallace

Text by Paul Dickson

Foreword by Lonnie G. Bunch

Founding Director, National Museum of African American

History and Culture, Smithsonian Institution

DOVER PUBLICATIONS, INC.

Mineola, New York

Library of Congress Cataloging-in-Publication Data
Wallace, Jim.
  Courage in the moment : the civil rights struggle,
1961-1964 / photographs by Jim Wallace ;
text by Paul Dickson.
    p. cm.
  Includes bibliographical references.
  ISBN-13: 978-0-486-47256-0
  ISBN-10: 0-486-47256-6
  1. Civil rights movements—North Carolina—Chapel Hill—
History—20th century—Pictorial works. 2. Civil rights
demonstrations—North Carolina—Chapel Hill—History
—20th century—Pictorial works. 3. African Americans
—North Carolina—Chapel Hill—History—20th century
—Pictorial works. 4. Chapel Hill (N.C.)—Race relations
—History—20th century—Pictorial works. I. Dickson, Paul.
II. Title.
  F264.C38W35 2012
  323.1196′0730756565—dc23

Bibliographical Note
*Courage in the Moment: The Civil Rights Struggle,
1961–1964*, is a new work, first published by Dover
Publications, Inc., in 2012.

Contributors
Publisher: Christopher J. Kuppig
Senior Editor: John Grafton
Publication Coordinator: Amy Pastan
Designer: Linda McKnight, McKnight Design, LLC
Project Manager: Janet B. Kopito
Copy Editor: Suzanne Fox

Manufactured in the United States
by Courier Corporation
47256601
www.doverpublications.com

Frontispiece. A march organized by the Chapel Hill
Freedom Movement on Franklin Street, Chapel Hill's
main thoroughfare. Protesters stopped to point out
segregated establishments.

Contents

xii   Foreword

xvii   Acknowledgments

2   The Day Jim Wallace Un-boxed His Negatives

8   From the Top—On Assignment in Chapel Hill

14   Pickets, Sit-ins, and Police

34   The Speaker Ban and Other Hurdles

52   The March on Washington and Its Aftermath

70   Access Denied—Officially

78   Mass Protest / Civil Disobedience / Human Chains

90   The Ku Klux Klan Reacts

100   The Struggle Continued and Resolved

105   Chronology

107   After Chapel Hill

108   Notes on the Photographs

109   Sources

Marchers with the Chapel Hill Freedom Movement point to a segregated restaurant.

Opposite. Supporters of a Chapel Hill public accommodations ordinance pack the First Baptist Church. *Daily Tar Heel* reporter Joel Bulkley (in sweater and collared shirt) stands at front left.

Right. Chapel Hill policemen Coy Durham (left) and Amos Horn (right) carry Johnnie Perry to a police car. Perry was participating in a sit-in protesting segregation at Brady's Restaurant.

Members of the Ku Klux Klan parade past a burning cross.

Foreword

*"The whole history of the progress of human liberty shows that all concessions...
have been born of earnest struggle. If there is no struggle, there is no progress."*

Frederick Douglass, *My Bondage and My Freedom,* 1855

On an extremely hot August day in the summer of 2011, I was walking along the National Mall in Washington, D.C., heading towards the newly opened Martin Luther King, Jr. National Memorial. It was impossible not to think about another humid day forty-eight years earlier when thousands traveled from all over America to participate in the March on Washington. There they were electrified by Dr. King's "I Have a Dream" speech, a speech that transfixed the nation and transformed the struggle for racial equality from a "southern problem" into one of national and international prominence and importance. As I entered the newest monument in the nation's capital, I quickly forgot about the controversies surrounding the memorial: Should it have been designed by an American? Did the image of Dr. King appear too austere? Why did the sculpted figure seem unfinished? These questions disappeared, not as the result of the power of the memorial, but because of the amazing array of people, a wonderfully multiracial crowd, all whom gathered to celebrate the life and legacy of a man who has come to symbolize the American civil rights movement. Yet as families posed their children in front of the memorial or as individuals ran their hands over the carved words of many of King's most important speeches, I wondered if they understood the enormity of the struggle—the actions and sacrifices of individuals and communities that changed our country for the better. I wondered if they knew just how revolutionary this gathering would have been in 1954, when the Supreme Court considered the legality of school segregation in *Brown v. Board of Education.*

America today is a profoundly different nation than it was in the mid-twentieth century. Much of that transformation is a result of the struggle to force this country to acknowledge its tortured racial past and to confront the racial inequities that were an everyday fact of life in Jim Crow America. It is a struggle that the photography of Jim Wallace captures beautifully and evocatively in *Courage in the Moment: The Civil Rights Struggle, 1961-1964*. It is difficult for many to remember, or for others to believe, just how much race shaped the possibilities of millions and touched all aspects of American life, from politics to religion, to the economy, to entertainment, to foreign policy. Race cast such a large shadow that this nation is still grappling with the effects and legacy of attitudes and policies that were embraced by many generations.

Throughout much of the twentieth century, a time when most African Americans either lived in the South or were one generation removed from their southern roots, segregation was the law of the land. An amazingly large thicket of laws and customs was created to ensure that racial lines were not crossed when it came to accommodations, restaurants, social activities, workplaces, marriages, and even final resting places. And transgressions along the color line were met by threats to one's employment, harassment, intimidation, and often by violence and death. In 1958 Dr. King crystallized the omnipresent specter and impact of segregation when he wrote, "I had grown up abhorring not only segregation but also the oppressive and barbarous acts that grew out of it. I had passed spots where men had been savagely lynched, and had watched the Ku Klux Klan on its rides at night. I had seen police brutality with my own eyes." To ensure that government protected and enforced this system of overt discrimination, the right to vote, the right to exercise one of the key tenets of democracy, was denied to thousands of African Americans. Throughout the South, counties and precincts with significant black populations used a variety of methods from outright intimidation to economic coercion and imposed poll taxes and literacy tests to guarantee that the political voice of the black community was silenced.

Thankfully for America, thousands of citizens refused to let racism silence them. In many ways, the post-World War II struggle for racial equality, known as the Freedom Movement by those intimately involved in this battle, was fueled by the courage and the commitment to speak truth to power—regardless of the costs and consequences. Yet this struggle was shaped by earlier strategies and acts of defiance that began when the first enslaved Africans refused to give up their dreams of freedom. This movement built on a tradition of protest and an expectation that America would live up to its founding ideals, a tradition that was an integral part of the African American experience. This movement owed much to earlier actions, such as the 1930s struggle to improve economic opportunities for blacks through boycotting discriminatory business in a national campaign encapsulated by the slogan "Don't Buy Where You Cannot Work," and the efforts by African American women in places like Alabama and Mississippi to expose and to confront crimes of rape and sexual violence that were such a part of life in Jim Crow America. Even the wonderful oratory of Dr. King and other movement leaders such as Bob Moses, Fanny Lou Hammer, Roy Wilkins, and Whitney Young echo the words and beliefs of earlier generations of leaders like Frederick Douglass, Mary McLeod Bethune, and W. E. B. DuBois.

So much of our knowledge and our memories of the civil rights struggle have been informed by a visual iconography that emphasizes the role of leaders such as Dr. King and focuses much of our attention on climatic moments such as the Selma marches, the protests in Birmingham, and the March on Washington. Yet the struggle for equality took place in hundreds of hamlets, urban corners, farming communities, and areas too small to name or to remember. And while the leadership helped to articulate and make manifest this movement on the national stage, so much of the battle was led and carried by thousands in overalls and well-worn dresses who neither sought nor achieved fame or notoriety.

Courage in the Moment helps us remember just how great the challenge was and to remember those who walked, sat-in, and were arrested—all in the cause of fairness and freedom. *Courage in the Moment* also reminds us that one of the key factors in the ultimate success of this movement was the ability to gain the nation's attention through the visual media of television and photography. The strategic brilliance of the freedom struggle was the recognition that the visual media was a crucial weapon that was stronger than the dogs, water hoses, and clubs used to enforce segregation, and more powerful than all the racist rhetoric of men like "Bull" Connor, Lester Maddox, and George Wallace. By ensuring that moments of bravery and moments of tragedy were captured on film, the movement leaders understood that the actions of those who discriminated and hated would no longer remain hidden, and that all of America would have to confront the shameful treatment and the bigotry in its midst. Ultimately, leaders like King and photographers like Jim Wallace knew that there were few things as powerful as an image that reveals truths, that stirs our emotions, that captures courage, and that serves as a call to action.

I remember quite clearly the day I received a call from Jim Wallace asking if I would be interested in seeing some of his photographs from the 1960s. As the founding director of the

Smithsonian Institution's newest museum, the National Museum of African American History and Culture, I receive a dizzying number of calls from photographers, but I never hesitated to meet with Jim. Jim Wallace had been a valued colleague of mine at the Smithsonian for more than twenty years. His photographic skills and goodwill had rescued me more times than I care to admit. Over the years of our association, I had seen many of Jim's photographs so I thought I knew much of his portfolio. I must admit that when he brought many of the images that comprise *Courage in the Moment* into my office, I was stunned. As Jim discussed each photograph I became more excited not only by the extraordinary visual quality of the images but also by their content. Before the meeting had ended I knew that many of these images needed to become part of the permanent collection of the museum. Fortunately for me, Jim agreed.

So what was it about this work that moved me so? First, I was struck by the period in which the images were shot. This was a key moment in American history. It marked the beginning of the administration of President Kennedy. With Kennedy's election came a renewed hope that the federal government would take a more active role in protecting the civil rights of all of its citizens, including African Americans. This was also a moment when the movement began to receive consistent national attention through the coverage it garnered in the media thanks to events like the Freedom Rides, James Meredith's integration of the University of Mississippi, the passage of the Civil Rights Act of 1964 and, of course, the March on Washington. In essence, Jim's work chronicled one of the most interesting and important eras in the long history of the struggle for equal rights in America. I was also struck by much of his work documenting many of the movement activities in North Carolina. These important images help us have a fuller and richer understanding of how the freedom struggle was comprised of moments known and unknown led by individuals whose courage and creativity undergirded and made possible the national visibility that was so essential to the success of the movement.

What made these images so moving and so haunting was the powerful intimacy that Jim Wallace captured. We have all seen the strong images of the March on Washington. While Jim Wallace's work is important because it adds to the corpus of images and knowledge about that crucial moment, his work also brings a freshness that I found surprising. His photography of that day captures the iconic shots of the crowds and the Lincoln Memorial, but what impressed me was his ability to help us see beyond the crowds into the faces of the participants. The image of a young interracial couple cooling off by the Reflecting Pool at the end of this book helps bring the event to a more human scale. It is an image that hints at a future where race would no longer be an unbridgeable divide.

For me, the power of Jim's photography is best reflected in his images of the Ku Klux Klan. These are amazing images on so many levels. The openness and confidence of the Klan members helps us remember that not too long ago that kind of intimidation, violence, and lawlessness was an accepted part of life in many communities throughout the nation. Yet it is the image of the Klan members circling a large burning cross that is seared into my memory. I can feel the heat and the hatred as if I were there. Few images capture an era as powerfully and as simply. I remember being a ten-year-old child sitting in the back seat of my parents' car as we drove home to New Jersey after visiting relatives in North Carolina. I was almost asleep when my father slammed on the brakes and speedily reversed the car. As he raced down a different road, I asked what had happened. He said he saw the Klan burning a cross ahead and that for our own safety we had to take another way home. Looking at the photographs taken by Jim Wallace, I now know what I had not seen that night so many years ago. As a historian of race, I have seen hundreds, if not thousands, of images of the Ku Klux Klan but none will stay with me as long as the photographs in *Courage in the Moment.*

America was made better by the postwar struggle for freedom. And thanks to the publication of *Courage in the Moment: The Civil Rights Struggle, 1961-1964,* we are fortunate to have access to Jim Wallace's images and memories, which will enhance our understanding of a pivotal and difficult time in our history.

Lonnie G. Bunch
Founding Director
National Museum of African American History and Culture
Smithsonian Institution

Acknowledgments

Someone once said that the secret to photojournalism is "f/11, and be there." While that may have been the key to many of the photographs in this book, I had a lot of help with "being there." My parents paid all the bills—four years at an out-of-state university, plus numerous summer sessions—while they watched my grades hover below average. I sent them a mail subscription to *The Daily Tar Heel* so they could keep up with, and probably worry about, what I was doing when I was not in class.

Editor Wayne King gave me my first civil rights assignment and led the paper's continuing coverage of the movement, as did the series of co-editors who were elected annually by the University of North Carolina student body and who followed him: Jim Clotfelter and Chuck Wrye, Gary Blanchard and David Etheridge, Hugh Stevens and Fred Seeley. We had an outstanding group of reporters. I worked mainly with Karen Parker, Peter Harkness, Mike Putzel, Joel Bulkley, and especially Mickey Blackwell. Mickey and I covered the KKK rally pictured in these pages together, and we once went to Greensboro the night before two final exams to cover a march.

In addition to the excellent faculty of the School of Journalism, the legendary editor Jim Shumaker taught me even more about journalism. I'd sit in his office at *The Chapel Hill Weekly* (where the *DTH* was printed) when I was night editor waiting for the press to run. I should have gotten several semesters' credit for what I gleaned from those conversations and his guidance.

It would have been impossible for me to take many of these photographs without the help of Chapel Hill Police Chief William Blake and Detective Lindy Pendergrass. While they were working to maintain calm in Chapel Hill, they gave me unprecedented access to the events depicted in these photographs. Outside the *DTH* office on campus, Harry's restaurant was a refuge for both *The Daily Tar Heel* staff and leaders of the movement. Unlike most other businesses in town, owners Harry and Sybil Macklin set examples by welcoming all races. And it was there and at the black churches that John Dunne, Pat Cusick, Quinton Baker, and others took me into their confidence, informing me of upcoming activities, which allowed me to be at the center of many scenes of the struggle. Almost fifty years later, Rob Stephens and the staff of the St. Joseph Christian Methodist Episcopal's Jackson Center held an open house for members of local churches to help me identify and gather histories of many of the people in the images.

This book was born at the National Press Club in Washington. Keri Douglas, the exhibit committee chair, sponsored a display of forty of these photographs. Paul Dickson, whose enlightening text for this book provides historical context for the images, introduced me to Chris Kuppig and John Grafton of Dover Publications. Amy Pastan was my talented picture editor and Linda McKnight the wonderful designer—the result you hold in your hands.

The Press Club exhibit and the book would not have happened without the continuing assistance from my wife, Jolleen. She has kept me organized and focused, and has been there every step of the way, including at the St. Joseph's open house. She is the best critic and editor I have.

Finally, I owe my thanks to the people you see in these photographs—picketing, marching, sitting-in, being arrested, and risking prison. They tried against great odds to change their own town. Their courage continues to serve as an inspiring example for all of us.

—Jim Wallace

"There was an almost complete failure on the part of the press in reporting the Chapel Hill crisis. As a result, many North Carolinians and most of the rest of the nation had little idea that anything was happening there, much less anything of consequence."

—Wilma Dykeman, *The Chicago Tribune*, April 18, 1965

The Day Jim Wallace Un-boxed His Negatives

In 2006, at the age of sixty-three, photographer Jim Wallace became seriously ill and spent time in intensive care on the critical list before he could go home to make his slow recovery. Like many who have had a brush with their own mortality, Jim spent part of his recovery time taking inventory of his life, so far. Very important items in that inventory were the civil rights images he had taken as a student photographer at the University of North Carolina, Chapel Hill, in the early 1960s while working for the student newspaper, *The Daily Tar Heel*.

During his four years at the paper, Wallace had taken hundreds of rolls of 35mm film, primarily of athletic events and student activities. As he recalls, "I was the main and often only photographer for the paper, and we published six days a week. I had field passes to photograph every home football game, I photographed every home Carolina basketball game from the floor, as well as every ACC tournament if UNC was playing. When entertainers like Pete Seeger and Peter, Paul, and Mary, came to UNC-Chapel Hill for concerts at Memorial Hall, I photographed them. There were also politicians and other dignitaries, including President Kennedy. I still have all of those negatives."

But these were not the images Wallace was drawn back to. The photographs in question were those he took documenting what the people involved in it called the "struggle"—the fight for equal accommodation: the right to sit down at lunch counters

A protest march makes its way from St. Joseph's CME Church to Franklin Street, passing policeman Coy Durham. To maintain calm, the Chapel Hill police often treated the marches as parades.

and order a cup of coffee. Wallace had long planned to go through the film, but now the time was right. The negatives, wound tight in hair-curler-sized rolls, needed to be unfurled, laid into strips, and housed in protective archival sleeves from which contact prints could be made. Only then could the most important images be edited, digitally scanned, and printed.

Wallace, who had spent twenty-nine years of his professional life as the Director/Curator of the Office of Imaging and Photographic Services at the Smithsonian Institution in Washington, had long been a member of the National Press Club. He decided to enter four of his civil rights photos in the club's annual members' photography exhibit. The images so moved the club's exhibits committee chair, Keri Douglas, that Wallace was invited to stage a full-fledged mezzanine exhibit entitled *Eat at Joe's Black + White*. It featured forty of his photographs documenting civil rights marches, sit-ins, arrests, the Ku Klux Klan, and the 1963 March on Washington. Only a few of the images had ever been seen by the public.

The forty images selected, printed, and captioned by Wallace not only attracted the attention of club members but also captivated those who used the facility for other functions. One night, a small group of African Americans attending a wedding there began looking at the photographs. They were overheard discussing the enormity of what had been captured in these forty black-and-white images, and the guts it had taken to shoot them.

It became clear that not only were these remarkable images, but also that they deserved to be seen and appreciated by a much wider audience. The first major step was Wallace's donation of thirty-six images to the permanent collection of the Smithsonian's new National Museum of African American History and Culture in Washington. The second was the decision by Dover Publications to publish this visual record of his courage and that of the people he photographed.

In 2010, while selecting the images for this book, Wallace returned to Chapel Hill. St. Joseph's CME Church had arranged an open house for members of the community to view the photographs Wallace shot nearly fifty years before and help identify the demonstrators pictured. During the event, Wallace was struck by the universal reaction from the younger people reviewing the photographs—something like, "I'd always heard about this, but never really saw it like this before." The photographs prompted them to ask the older generation, "What did you do during the struggle?" They were surprised by the answers and proud when they recognized family and friends among the faces of those who tried to change history.

Marchers protesting segregated facilities stop in front of Clarence's Bar and Grill, while owner Clarence Grey and patrons of the restaurant gather at the front door to watch.

From the Top—
On Assignment in Chapel Hill

Jim Wallace arrived in Chapel Hill in the fall of 1960 with a Miranda D 35mm camera and three cheap lenses, 28mm, 135mm, and 300mm. He had started taking pictures at Falls Church High School in Virginia and had learned tricks useful to a young photographer on a limited budget. He bought his film in bulk 100-foot rolls and loaded it into the canisters that fit into the camera. By loading more than the commercial twenty or thirty-six exposures he could squeeze in a few extra shots per roll.

It would be years before he could afford a higher-end Nikon, and the Miranda remained his camera throughout his college years. By current standards, it was primitive and labor-intensive. Wallace explains, "There was no light meter. You pre-set the shutter speed and f/stop. Then you focus with the lens wide open, move a lever that stops the aperture down, and then press the shutter release."

If the camera was basic, the film was even more so. Wallace disliked flashbulb photography ("flashbulbs cost money and draw unwanted attention when they fire. But there were times at night when you just had to use them"). That meant he needed the fastest film on the market. For the next four years, he would exclusively shoot Kodak black-and-white Tri-X film, which was normally rated at 400 ASA but could be pushed higher in the darkroom by letting it develop longer. If there was a drawback to Tri-X, it was that it was grainier than its first cousin, Plus-X.

At the University of North Carolina, Chapel Hill, Wallace enrolled in the School of

Clementine Farrington leads demonstrators. Marchers almost always carried the American flag, but not the North Carolina flag, during their protests.

Journalism and Mass Communication, hoping to turn his fascination for things visual into a career in photojournalism or television. In the second semester of his freshman year, he headed for the student newspaper, *The Daily Tar Heel,* where he was immediately welcomed.

When Chi Omega sorority and the ATO fraternity held banquets at the segregated Pines Restaurant, they were picketed by their fellow students.

The Daily Tar Heel had been in business since 1893 and had a long and illustrious history. Novelist Thomas Wolfe was its editor in 1920, and he converted the newspaper from a weekly to a bi-weekly. It became a daily in 1929. When Wallace arrived, the outgoing editor was Jonathan Yardley, a future Pulitzer Prize winner and book critic for the *Washington Post.* Yardley turned over the reins to Wayne King, who hired Jim Wallace.

Wallace recalls that *The Daily Tar Heel* was an editor's dream because the staff was given the freedom to make it a totally independent voice. "It was unusual for many student newspapers of the time, in that we did not have a faculty advisor, we did not have any faculty oversight, there was no dean, who would say that you can't print this, or you can't print that, or you can't do whatever. It got some monies from student fees, it sold advertising, and the leaders of the University saw what was in the daily paper at the same time everybody else did. And so, it left us very open to be able to cover what was going on without having to look over our shoulders." This freedom attracted talented student editors and reporters. [In November 1994, the paper posted its first edition online, becoming one of the first newspapers in the country to do so.]

For Wallace, the paper was his entrée into journalism. Soon, his role expanded beyond *The Daily Tar Heel.* "After I started working for the student newspaper, I also became a stringer for United Press International, and later *Newsweek* and *The Charlotte*

Observer." He recalled how he became a stringer for UPI. "While photographing events, I had met the photographer from UPI who covered North Carolina, a photojournalist named Joe Holloway. Joe was photographing the civil rights movement along with everything else in North Carolina. . . . He was the only UPI photographer in the state. He helped me become a member of the student affiliate of the National Press Photographers Association, and he was looking for a stringer in Chapel Hill to cover for him when he was elsewhere. I'd make prints for him and put them on a Trailways bus to Raleigh."

The Trailways bus station was central to life in Chapel Hill, which lacked a railroad station. For Jim Wallace, it was his means of traveling home to Virginia for the holidays because he did not have a car. The bus was also a reminder of the struggle at hand in Chapel Hill and other parts of the South because it was segregated. As Wallace recalls: "Whites sat in front, and blacks were in the back."

Carrying an American flag, Sharmine Baldwin leads
marchers who are demanding integration via the
passage of a Chapel Hill public accommodations law.

Above. Albert Amon, an assistant professor of psychology at UNC. He regularly accompanied evening protesters demonstrating at segregated businesses. He was severely kicked and beaten at a sit-in at a restaurant outside Chapel Hill. Several months later he died from a brain aneurism. A direct connection between his beating and death was never officially made.

Right. Albert Amon leads picketers at the Rialto Theater in Durham in the spring of 1963.

Opposite. A march on Independence Day, July 4, 1964, through downtown Chapel Hill.

Pickets, Sit-ins, and Police

O n February 1, 1960, a new word entered the American lexicon when the first "sit-in" with national news coverage was staged at a lunch counter in a Greensboro, North Carolina, Woolworth's variety store. Four students from the North Carolina Agricultural and Technical College sat down and ordered coffee at the store's "whites only" lunch counter. Denied service, they sat at the counter and read until the store closed. On the second day, twenty students showed up, along with the national media. On the third day, there were sixty, and by the fourth, more than 300 showed up and took seats at Woolworth's and also at a nearby Kress variety store. The demonstrators carried posters. The one that was most quoted in the press played on America's cold war with the Soviet Union: "KHRUSHCHEV CAN EAT HERE BUT WE CAN'T."

This simple act of defiance reverberated throughout the Jim Crow South and across the nation, motivating others to engage in civil disobedience to push for equal treatment of all Americans, regardless of race. These were non-violent events led by students who dressed as they would for church, and they masked their anger with politeness. Sympathy was widespread, and their supporters included no less a figure than President Dwight D. Eisenhower, who said as the sit-ins spread that he supported the students and expressed his sympathy for those who were fighting for their human and civil rights, adding that he was "deeply sympathetic with efforts of any group to enjoy the rights. . . of equality that they are guaranteed by the Constitution."

Demonstrators, including Walter Mitchell (center), are arrested during a night sit-in blocking the door to Colonial Drug. Members of owner John Carswell's family and a friend watch from inside.

In Chapel Hill, John Carswell, a 1943 graduate of the university, was the owner of Colonial Drug, which stood at 450 West Franklin Street near the unofficial border between the white and black communities. Whites got full service at the fountain and lunch counter, while blacks wanting a milk shake or a sandwich had to use the back door. To this day, blacks who once frequented the store are convinced that the prices were the same for both races, but that their portions were smaller.

On February 28, 1960, a small group of young black students from Lincoln High School sat down in a booth at Colonial Drug. When they were denied service, they refused to leave. They were arrested and charged with trespassing. Intense picketing campaigns soon followed outside Colonial Drug and the nearby segregated Long Meadow Dairy Bar, Bus Station Grill, and Village Pharmacy. The integration movement in Chapel Hill was underway. As it was elsewhere throughout the South, "The Movement" was rooted in the African American churches. The black churches were places where the organizers could meet. More white students were among the demonstrators there than in other areas because Chapel Hill had always had a reputation for being the liberal seat of the South. Patrick Cusick, representing the UNC Student Peace Union, began a solitary picket of the College Café on Franklin Street. Another white student, John Dunne, perhaps most well-known among the student leaders, soon joined the picketing, which quickly spread to other establishments.

But the strength of the movement came from local black churches, mainly St. Joseph's Christian Methodist Episcopal (CME) and the First Baptist Church. Local African American youths formed the Chapel Hill Council on Racial Equality. Chapel Hill resident Harold Foster was selected to be the chair of the executive committee. Other leaders included Hilliard Caldwell (later elected to the Carrboro Board of Aldermen) and James Foushee. Together with a scattering of UNC students, the marchers and picketers were

March leaders address participants in front of St. Joseph's CME Church.

mainly students, women, and older men. Many black men reported that their jobs would be threatened if they openly joined the movement.

So when Jim Wallace arrived on campus as a freshman in the fall of 1960, there was already a small but vocal civil rights movement in Chapel Hill. Its original focus was to allow blacks to sit down at the tables, counters, and booths at segregated eating establishments and be served. It was a struggle for equal accommodations, pure and simple.

Wallace's first involvement came as an assignment from Wayne King, his editor at *The Daily Tar Heel.* King later went on to *The Detroit Free Press*, where he shared in a Pulitzer Prize for coverage of the 1967 Detroit riots, and *The New York Times,* where he was twice nominated for the Pulitzer. He then taught at Wake Forest University before retiring in 2011. Wallace remembers that King and the editors who came after him were all interested in covering the civil rights movement in the South, but especially in Chapel Hill: "Jim Clotfelter, who followed King as editor, sent reporter Mike Putzel to Ole Miss, where he was tear-gassed while covering the story about James Meredith's attempt to enroll there in 1962."

Wayne King and his successors decided in part that *The Daily Tar Heel* was going to cover the movement because it involved students. The University of North Carolina had some, not many, black students at that time, but mainly at the graduate school level. It was almost entirely a white male institution, with athletic teams that were all white. It would not be until 1966 that basketball star Charles Scott would become the first black scholarship athlete at UNC, but as Wallace puts it, "The fact that there were students at the University who couldn't use some of the facilities on Franklin Street, downtown, made it of interest to those of us who were working on the paper."

Wallace cannot remember the details of his first civil rights assignment from King— "It would have probably been picketing or a march of some kind. I don't specifically remember the absolute first assignment"—but he was soon deeply involved. The demonstrators were quick to realize how important Wallace and his photographs were to their cause, which cried out for documentation.

Wallace would often meet with the demonstrators' leaders and be told in advance about the day's events at one of the few fully integrated eating places in Chapel Hill. It was a New York-style delicatessen called Harry's, operated by Harry and Sybil Macklin. Harry's was one of Chapel Hill's most popular gathering places for the liberal community. Wallace was partial to Harry's for other reasons as well, "I had never had real New York delicatessen food. It was where I learned to eat pastrami and corned beef and the like—and love it."[1]

[1]Wallace adds: "And Harry's was one of the few places that would let you run up a tab. So we could eat at Harry's and then at the first of the month, we could pay off the tab." Harry's was so popular that two decades later, Wallace and more than 100 others attended a reunion, "From the Tables Down at Harry's," on the rock wall across Franklin Street from where the restaurant had been.

In 1963, CORE leader Floyd McKissick asked Quinton Baker, one of his most trusted organizers, to go to Chapel Hill and teach effective nonviolence tactics to local activists. Here Baker leads a practice protest march.

As the movement gathered momentum in Chapel Hill, a national movement was attracting much attention. In May 1961, the Congress of Racial Equality (CORE), led by James Farmer, organized integrated Freedom Rides to defy segregation in interstate bus transportation. Freedom riders were arrested in North Carolina and beaten in South Carolina. In Alabama, a bus was burned and the riders attacked with baseball bats and tire irons. Attorney General Robert Kennedy sent 400 federal marshals to protect the freedom riders and urged the Interstate Commerce Commission to order the desegregation of interstate travel. The university's attitude toward students who were participating in the movement and the coverage in *The Daily Tar Heel* was one of neutrality. They did not openly support the students, but at the same time they did not discipline them.

[2] Pat Cusick, interview L-0043, June 19, 1989. Southern Oral History Program Collection (#4007) in the Southern Oral History Program Collection, Southern Historical Collection, Wilson Library, University of North Carolina at Chapel Hill.

[3] Jim Wallace, interview with Lindy Pendergrass, July 9, 2010.

Unlike in many parts of the South, the Chapel Hill movement didn't face a hostile police force. Student Patrick Cusick once said that Police Chief William Blake was a formidable adversary to desegregation demonstrators, but it was not because of any violent tactic he employed; rather, it was because he was well versed in the philosophy of civil disobedience. According to Cusick, Chief Blake had been reading works by Mahatma Gandhi since the 1940s. Blake, who headed an integrated police force, also recognized the effect that Wallace's news photographs could have on the minds of the general public. "He knew as much about nonviolent tactics as we did," Cusick said in a 1989 interview, "So he would not allow us to use his recalcitrance, like the whole scene in Birmingham and stuff. So once we said, 'Well, we're marching anyway,' he didn't arrest us. He then turned it into a parade for us, and that characterized his tactics throughout the movement."[2]

Lindy Pendergrass, then one of Blake's detectives and later long-term Sheriff of Orange County, noted that Blake told his men "…to treat the demonstrators like we wanted to be treated ourselves." He added, "Two-thirds of the people who you are arresting are people who you are going to have to live with for the rest of your lives." He recalled: "Chief Blake was adamant about the fact that there would be no fire hoses, no dogs…none of that stuff."[3] As Wallace's coverage of the movement continued, Pendergrass helped the young photographer gain access inside the police lines during the arrests and even inside the station house.

What happened over time was that Wallace's news photography began to serve a purpose for both the police and the demonstrators. "I needed to get there just after they started a sit-in and before they were arrested," says Wallace of the demonstrators. "They needed me to be there to take photographs. My presence helped keep things cool." For the police, Wallace was the man who could lead them to the demonstrations in a timely manner, as well as provide documentation of events should they be needed later to show that the police had followed proper procedures in arresting the demonstrators.

For their part, the demonstrators employed the nonviolent tactic of going limp when apprehended by the police as a way to refrain from actively resisting arrest. "That meant they would not *resist* being arrested," says Wallace, "but they also would not *assist* being arrested. It took several police officers to carry them out of where they were sitting-in. The entire time they were always singing 'Freedom Songs.' But they all had to agree before a sit-in that they would not fight back or resist or whatever, no matter what was done to them."

This agreement, as Wallace recalled, "was not a 'raise-your-hand' oath, but it was just telling people that if you were going to do this, these were the rules and you had to practice passive resistance….Wayne King tells a story that he was actually picketing one day, and somebody came up and gave him a hard time and called him some names. Wayne turned to them and said that he didn't know what they thought but that he wasn't one of those passive resistance guys and he better watch what he was doing. The leaders of the movement pulled Wayne off the picket line right away and never let him actively participate again."

The demonstrations continued through the spring of 1963, with Wallace documenting it all for *The Daily Tar Heel* as tactics changed. Wallace remembers, "Movement organizers tried talking to these people, and they tried petitions and boycotts. When none of that worked, they began marching. They would march, generally not blocking traffic, and the marches varied in size. They were always singing, and they always carried the American flag, and were always well dressed," says Wallace. There were always songs.

"We Shall Overcome" was the anthem of the civil rights movement, but there were also a number of other songs including "What Side Are You On?" and "Paul and Silas Bound in Jail." The situation was not entirely grim, as some progress was being made. A story circulated that when a black cook at a segregated restaurant saw protesters outside the establishment, he told the owner, "Those are my people out there," and said he was going to quit. To keep the cook, the restaurant owner integrated on the spot.

Meanwhile, in a nationally televised address on June 6, 1963, President John F. Kennedy urged the nation to take action toward guaranteeing equal treatment of every American regardless of race. Kennedy's message and the ongoing local demonstrations caused one Chapel Hill proprietor to dig in his heels and proclaim his continued resistance in a manner loud and clear. On June 12, 1963, John Carswell took out a full-page advertisement in the *Chapel Hill Weekly*, with this declaration: "We will not be Intimidated or Coerced by Certain Alphabetical Organizations or Committees under the Disguise of 'Betterment of Certain Groups or Races.'" A copy of the advertisement hung in the front window of his store, Colonial Drug.

Soon after his televised address, Kennedy proposed that Congress consider civil rights legislation that would address voting rights, public accommodations, school desegregation, nondiscrimination in federally assisted programs, and more.

Chapel Hill Police Lt. Graham Creel (left) and John Nesbitt (right) stand between civil rights demonstrators and counter-protesters at Colonial Drug.

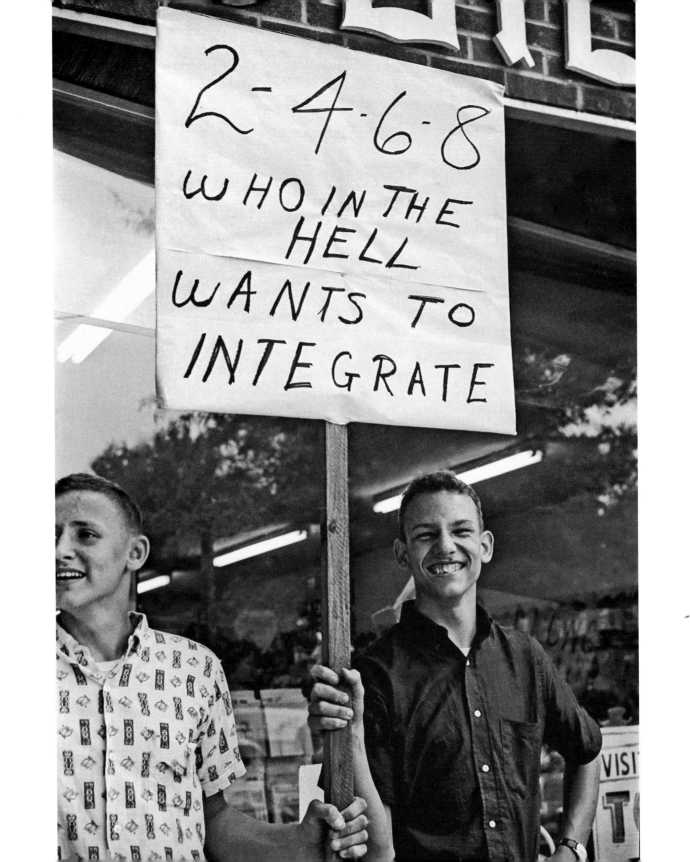

Opposite. Boys stage a counter-protest directed at marchers at the segregated Colonial Drug.

Right. Marchers on Franklin Street protest at segregated Colonial Drug.

THE CUSTOMER IS ALWAYS WHITE AT COLONIAL'S LUNCH COUNTER'S BOOTHS

Opposite. A UNC representative of the Student Peace
Union pickets the segregated College Café.

Above. Demonstrators gather at St. Joseph's CME
Church before marching through Chapel Hill, where
they stopped to protest at each segregated business.

Young student marchers, both black and white, point accusingly at segregated businesses in Chapel Hill.

Opposite. Harold Foster rallies demonstrators in front of St. Joseph's CME Church before marching through Chapel Hill.

Above. Demonstrators congregate at St. Joseph's CME Church before a march. Reinvigorated by the March on Washington, activists rallied across the country, including in Chapel Hill, where participants often numbered in the hundreds.

Picketers at the University Motel, just outside Chapel Hill.

As they march from St. Joseph's CME Church toward downtown Chapel Hill, local African American students, religious leaders, and UNC students rally behind a banner declaring "Eat at Joe's Black & White."

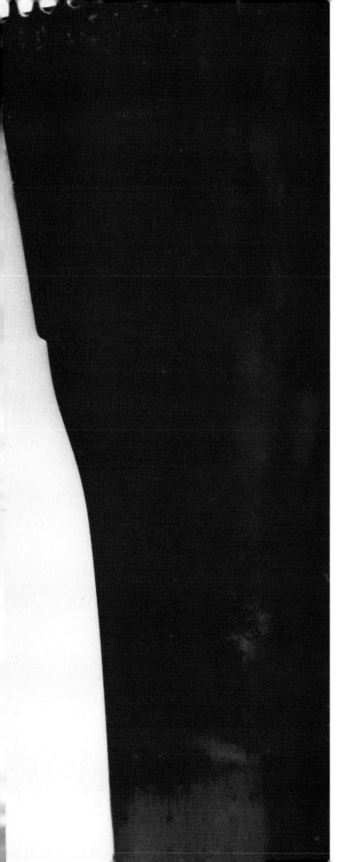

The Speaker Ban and Other Hurdles

North Carolina Governor Terry Sanford was determined that his state would not suffer the racial violence seen in Alabama and Mississippi. On July 3, 1963, he met in Raleigh with black leaders from throughout the state. Wallace photographed the meeting. He remembers, "The group from Chapel Hill included Harold Foster, one of the local leaders. It was important—the first governor of a southern state meeting with the civil rights movement."

Days later, Sanford met with mayors and public officials from across the state. They formed the North Carolina Mayors Cooperating Committee, which published a book titled *North Carolina and the Negro* that outlined racial relations in each of their jurisdictions. "The governor's office had been following our coverage in *The Daily Tar Heel*," Wallace notes. "They used several of my Chapel Hill photographs in the book."

On June 26, 1963, North Carolina legislative leaders orchestrated the quick passage of what came to be known as North Carolina's Speaker Ban Bill. It forbade individuals who were known to be members of the Communist Party or had invoked the Fifth Amendment in connection with Congressional investigations of Communist activities from speaking on the campuses of the University of North Carolina. The Speaker Ban Law was also generally considered a means of thwarting the civil rights marches that were taking place in Raleigh and other places in the state. It was a signal—an omen, perhaps—that certain officials were prepared to deal harshly with those demanding change.

A slogan painted on the door of a truck in Carrboro,
the town bordering Chapel Hill.

Top, left to right. North Carolina Governor Terry Sanford addresses the conference he organized in Raleigh on July 3, 1963, to discuss the "Negro Protest Movement." It marked the first time a Southern governor met with black leaders during the protests against segregation. General Capus M. Waynick, consultant on race relations to Governor Sanford, discusses plans with a participant at the conference. Jesse Jackson questions General Waynick.

Bottom, left to right. Civil rights leader Floyd McKissick attended the conference, as did Harold Foster, one of the leaders of the Chapel Hill Freedom Movement.

Opposite. Demonstrators gather on the steps of the North Carolina State Capitol at the conference to discuss the "Negro Protest Movement," July 3, 1963.

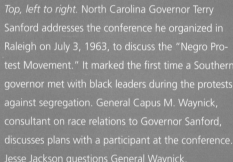

Less than a month later, on July 29, 1963, a sit-in was held at the Chapel Hill/Carr-boro Merchants Association. It was the largest demonstration to date and the first large scale sit-in. Jim Wallace was there: "Rather than picking an individual merchant, they tried to put pressure on the Chamber of Commerce and the Merchants Association, feel-ing that if they could get the Merchants Association to agree, then it would be easier to get the individual restaurants to agree. And again, all these people were looking for was the right to go in and sit down and eat. As an auxiliary to it all, at some point, there were several motels and restaurants on the edge of town and those were included in some of the picketing and the marches. But the main focus was to open all of the res-taurants in town. The sit-in at the Merchants Association brought the first large number of arrests." Thirty-four protesters were arrested and charged with trespassing, including Cusick and Dunne. Wallace's photos depicted the protesters' tactic of going limp, but this time on a much larger scale.

It was an active summer for Wallace, who was not only covering the movement in Chapel Hill but had also been in Raleigh and Durham photographing some of the marches there. He photographed segregationist Governor George Wallace (no relation) when he spoke in Durham a couple of times. In August 1963, Wallace boarded a bus to Virginia, drawn by an event that was tailor-made for a young photojournalist covering the civil rights movement. It was a culmination of the struggle people were waging in Chapel Hill: The March on Washington for Jobs and Freedom.

There was added significance to Jim Wallace boarding a Trailways bus heading north that day. In April 1947, civil rights pioneer Bayard Rustin had refused to move to the back of a Trailways bus in Chapel Hill and was arrested. Rustin was traveling and sitting where he chose because of a 1946 Supreme Court decision that declared that the ra-cial segregation of passengers on interstate buses was an "undue burden on interstate

Chapel Hill police officers David Caldwell, Coy Dur-ham, Charles Allison, and Herman Stone round up demonstrators for arrest at the Chapel Hill/Carrboro Merchants Association sit-in.

commerce" and could no longer be enforced. Rustin and other "freedom riders" set out to test the law. When Rustin refused to change his seat, he and the white man sitting next to him were arrested on charges of disorderly conduct for refusing to obey the order of the bus driver.

Despite the U.S. Supreme Court's decision overturning segregation on interstate carriers, the arrests were upheld by the North Carolina Supreme Court. The prosecution argued that because the passengers were not traveling outside of the state that day, they were not interstate travelers and thus the Supreme Court decision did not apply. Bayard Rustin spent twenty-two days on a prison chain gang in Roxboro, North Carolina. In August 1963 he was chief organizer of the March on Washington.

Opposite. Before each sit-in, demonstrators had to agree to practice nonviolent resistance by going limp to neither assist nor resist arrest. Here, they lie on Franklin Street, awaiting transportation to jail.

Chapel Hill Freedom Movement leaders John Dunne (left) and Pat Cusick (right) are pulled into a police car after being arrested at the Merchants Association sit-in.

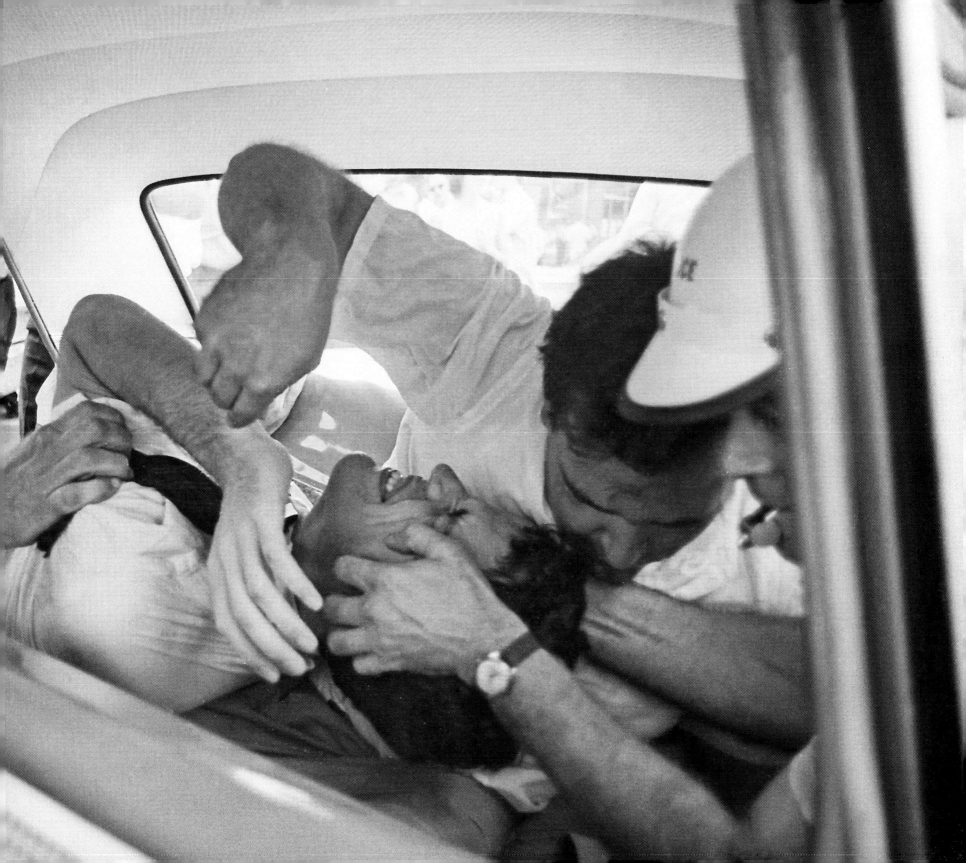

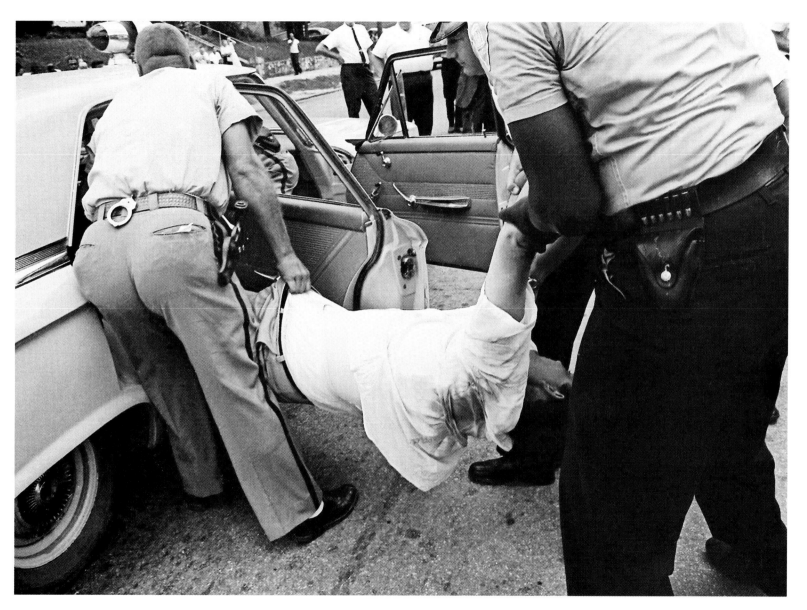

Opposite. Chapel Hill Police Detective Lindy Pendergrass carries Ruby Farrington to the police van following her arrest at a sit-in on Franklin Street.

Above. Police load a demonstrator into a car for transport to jail.

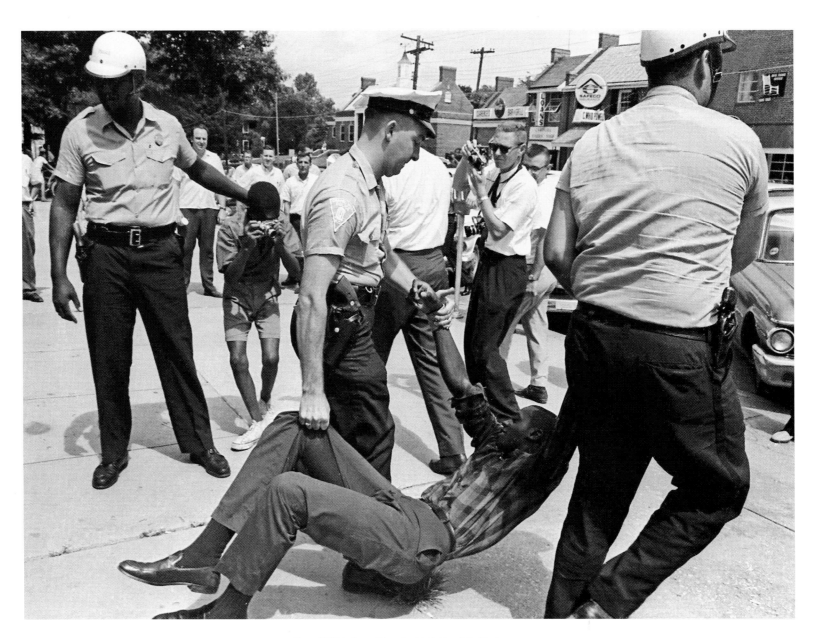

Chapel Hill Police officer David Caldwell (left) clears
the way for officer Earl Allen to carry a demonstrator
to a police car.

John Fykes sings as police drag him from the Merchants Association building sit-in. Demonstrators often sang freedom songs such as "We Shall Overcome" during their protests and arrests.

Chapel Hill police officers Graham Creel (left) and David Caldwell (right) carry Yvonne Cotton to a police car following her arrest for sitting-in at the Chapel Hill/Carrboro Merchants Association.

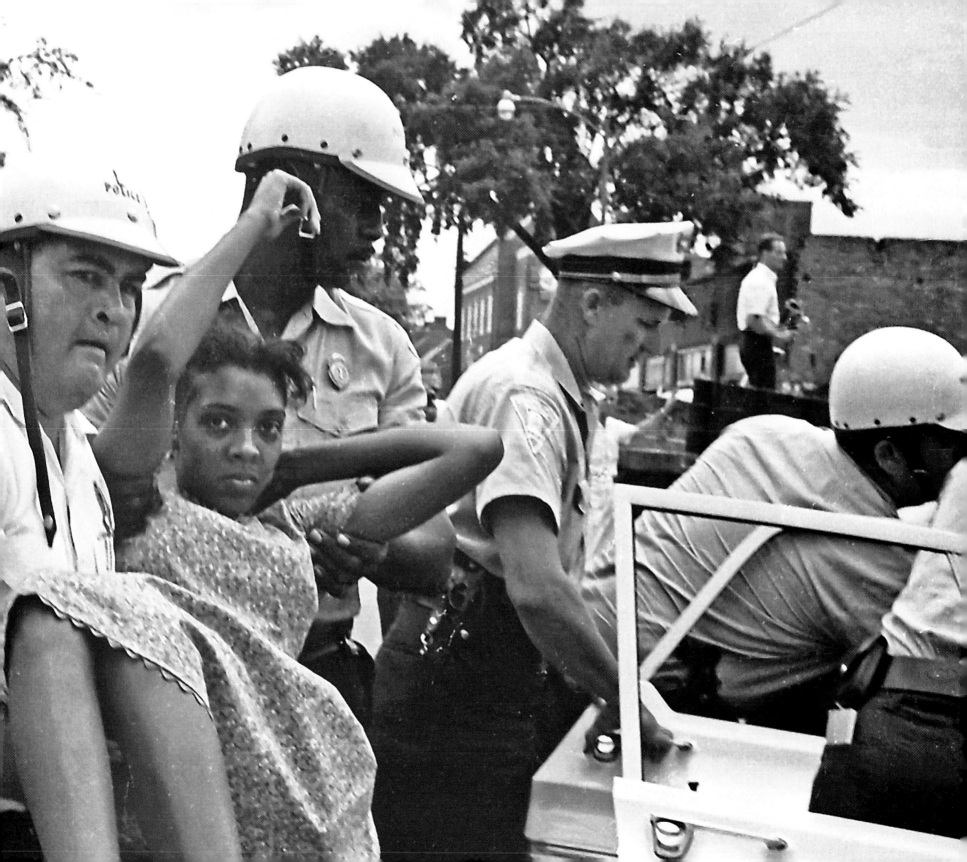

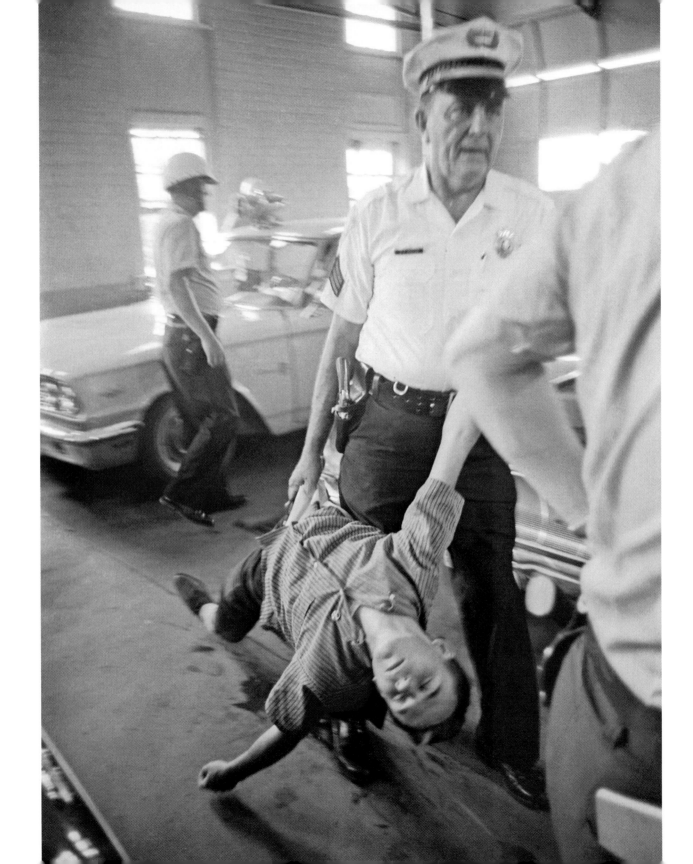

Opposite. A demonstrator arrested at the Merchants Association sit-in is carried through the garage in the Chapel Hill jail building.

Above. Chapel Hill Police Chief William Blake, with Officer Graham Creel (in helmet), warns the demonstrators to leave or they will be arrested. They were all arrested.

The March on Washington and Its Aftermath

On July 3, 1963, the Associated Press reported that a group led by Bayard Rustin and other Negro leaders had announced a civil rights march on Washington for August 28 that would be "...the strongest action, numerically speaking, that we have ever had." The Reverend Dr. Martin Luther King, Jr., president of the Southern Christian Leadership Conference, told the AP, "We'll have machinery that will control the demonstration. No acts that could be considered civil disobedience will occur."[1]

The news brought a quick reaction, which was not all positive. Arthur Spingarn, the eighty-five-year-old white head of the National Association for the Advancement of Colored People, had his doubts about the wisdom of the march and declared himself and his organization "not very enthusiastic." The following Sunday, the Reverend Dr. Lee A. Belford, a prominent Episcopal minister in Harlem, warned his parishioners against participating in the march because "tempers are bound to flare in the heat of a Washington summer and there is the danger that people will be injured and property destroyed." His comments were carried in the *New York Amsterdam News,* a leading African American newspaper.[2]

As opposition grew, King issued a statement: "There is no logical proof that this demonstration will not bring about success since we haven't gotten it anyway in the last 100 years." Even those on the right side of the civil rights struggle were unnerved by the

[1]*Hartford Courant*, July 3, 1963, 23.
[2]*New York Amsterdam News*, July 13, 1963, 20.

The March on Washington included participation not just by civil rights organizations, but by labor and religious organizations as well. Marchers from both the North and South called for a national public accommodations law.

[3]*Hartford Courant*, July 14, 1963, 2B.
[4]*The Washington Post*, Aug 27, 1963, B-1.

Left. An exuberant young boy is hoisted above the crowd.

Right. Walking up Constitution Avenue, a demonstrator announces his intention to run for the office of governor of Alabama.

concept of a large-scale march. "That massive March on Washington, planned for next month in support of the civil rights program in Congress, is intended as a peaceful one," read an editorial in the *Hartford Courant,* which then asked, "Will it be?" The writer added, "And even if it is, what will it achieve that has not already been achieved?"[3]

"I was determined to photograph the March on Washington," Wallace says. "It was one of the biggest events that had ever happened in Washington. They were going to have unprecedented crowds. So I was determined to cover it." But there were immediate concerns. The Army disclosed that about thirty helicopters were on their way from Fort Bragg, North Carolina, to provide rapid airlift for the 4,000 troops standing by in case they were needed to quell any disorder during the march. Pre-signed Executive Orders authorized military intervention in the case of rioting. All military bases in the area were closed for the day, and military personnel, black or white, were not allowed to attend the march even in civilian clothes. Some 350 Washington firemen were deputized as police for the event, suggesting that this was a demonstration that could not be handled by the police alone.[4]

The media sounded notes of caution. On the morning of the march, a nationally syndicated cartoon by Bill Mauldin depicted African Americans marching and holding banners as they walked toward and into an immense "Powder Keg"—a reflection of the segment of the American public that felt that the march would only incite further racial tensions. The cartoon appeared in *Raleigh News and Observer*, *Chicago Sun-Times*, and many other newspapers.

Despite the fears of his parents and the warnings of friends and neighbors (one of whom suggested he carry a baseball bat for his own safety), Wallace booked a room at the historic Willard Hotel at 14th and Pennsylvania Avenue NW, in downtown Washington. "My parents wanted me to stay in a good, safe place so they paid the bill," Wallace

A vendor sells pennants for the march on the
National Mall.

The march makes the front page.

More than 250,000 people gathered on the grounds of the Washington Monument for the March on Washington for Jobs and Freedom. At that time, it was the largest demonstration ever in the nation's capital.

recalls a half century later. "My guess is that the march had chased most regular customers out and most of the marchers were not staying at the Willard." As it turned out, Martin Luther King, Jr., was also staying at the Willard, where he completed the now-famous "I Have a Dream" speech he would deliver the next day.

"I had friends who said, 'Why are you going to do that, you're going to get hurt,'" Wallace recalls, "but I had been photographing marches and sit-ins all year. I thought it was fairly ludicrous for them to say that, but they hadn't been there, and I knew basically what I was getting into—a peaceful, planned event." Wallace was unable to get press credentials, which meant he did not get the iconic photograph of Martin Luther King looking out at the crowd toward the Washington Monument, but he did get pictures in the crowd and on the street. "Looking back on it, that was probably a better place to be," says Wallace, who was initially disappointed with the pictures he had taken because he had not been admitted to the speaker's platform.

Despite the fears that had prompted extraordinary precautions, an estimated quarter of a million people—about 60,000 of whom were white—marched from the Washington Monument to the Lincoln Memorial in what turned out to be both a protest and a communal celebration. "It was a huge crowd," Wallace recalls, "and it was a very well behaved crowd, they were all singing, there was a lot of representation from labor unions, black and some white fraternal organizations, churches, and synagogues. People were bused in from New York and elsewhere."

Asked if he ever felt threatened or apprehensive, Wallace responded: "It was a moving but happy event. The crowd was very upbeat. It was a celebration. After the march, I was glad I had a room downtown to avoid the crowds leaving the National Mall. I came back to the hotel and absolutely collapsed and woke up the next morning with the TV

After gathering at the Washington Monument grounds, the marchers walked up Constitution Avenue to the Lincoln Memorial. It was one of the first demonstrations in Washington covered by live television.

Young women and men sing freedom songs during the march.

Marchers gathered at the Lincoln Memorial, where
Dr. Martin Luther King, Jr., delivered his famous
"I Have a Dream" speech.

A tired demonstrator takes a break from the crowds and heat of the capital.

still on." For all the fears to the contrary, the event was noted for its civility and peacefulness. Wallace's images of the event reflect a racially integrated and orderly event that belies any sense of disharmony or tension. Wallace never published any of his images from the march. He developed the negatives and filed them away. It was not until he went back and looked at those negatives more than four decades later that he realized he had captured something special: a view of the march from the marcher's perspective.

"The March on Washington gave the Chapel Hill movement something more to build on," says Wallace. "It was now a bigger national thing, and if anything, it intensified the mood of some because they came back and were revitalized from being in Washington and seeing that they weren't just alone in their community and in their state, that this was, in fact, a big deal." The March on Washington reinvigorated the movement across the country, including activities in Chapel Hill, where participants in rallies and marches now often numbered in the hundreds. Jim Wallace was always out in front with his camera during these demonstrations.

There was also new blood in the Chapel Hill movement. Karen L. Parker had transferred to UNC-Chapel Hill as a journalism major, becoming the first black female undergraduate in the school's history. An ardent foe of segregation (as a child she had been denied access to a theater showing Walt Disney cartoons), Parker was arrested and jailed twice for participating in the sit-ins to integrate Chapel Hill businesses.

Her roommate was a white woman named Joanne Johnston-Francis, who was also committed to the movement and who was also arrested. After Jim Wallace's disturbing

Protesters sit-in at Carlton's Rock Pile, a whites-only convenience store. At another sit-in there on December 1, 1963, the owner doused a protester with ammonia.

Above. Orange County Sheriff's officers Avery Mad-drey (left) and Sylvester Thompson (right) carry Clyde Durham after he was arrested for sitting-in at Brady's Restaurant.

Right. Sit-in participants, singing and waving to the camera, block the door to Brady's Restaurant at the dinner hour. Chapel Hill Police Chief William Blake stands at right.

Opposite. Joanne Johnston-Francis is hauled by one arm after her arrest at a Brady's Restaurant sit-in.

photograph of a Chapel Hill police officer dragging her into custody by one arm was published [see photo, opposite] in *The Daily Tar Heel*, Chief Blake instructed his men henceforth to carry those being arrested. Parker still remembers the kindness of Chief Blake, who she says went out of his way to treat the demonstrators in a civil manner. The two women joined the growing movement of local townspeople as the frequency of the demonstrations increased. "We were out there night after night." Parker recalls. "It was constant."

Meanwhile, President Kennedy's comprehensive civil rights bill cleared several hurdles in Congress and won the endorsement of House and Senate Republican leaders. It was not passed, however, because on November 22, 1963, Kennedy was assassinated. As the year ended, the Chapel Hill civil rights activists seemed more determined than ever to succeed.

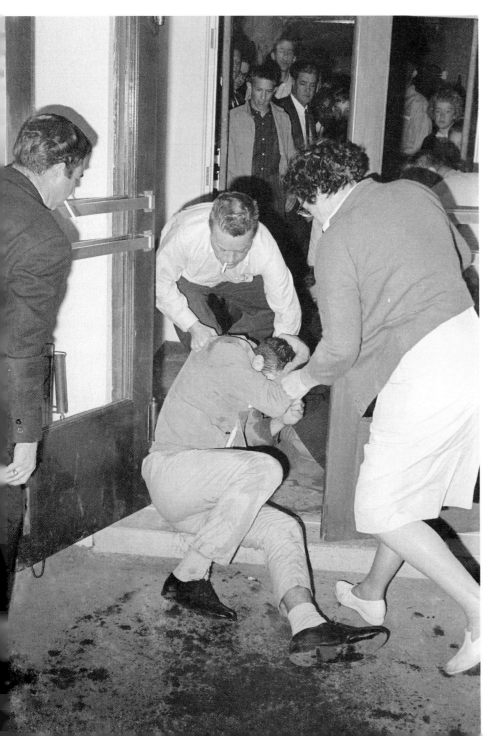

A demonstrator at Watts Restaurant is attacked
during a sit-in.

Perhaps no incidents did more to underscore the level of resistance faced by the demonstrators than the sit-ins at the Rock Pile, a convenience store "…where you had to be white to be able to buy anything or even to go in the door," recalls Wallace. "It had a big WHITES ONLY sign on the door." The Rock Pile was a frequent target of demonstrators. On December 1, 1963, a protester was doused with ammonia and cleaning fluid by the owner and had to be treated for first-degree burns at Memorial Hospital. The Rock Pile incident (which Wallace missed because he was out of town) brought on more demonstrations. "As it got more intense and as more and more people were arrested, made bail, and were out and got arrested again," remembers Wallace, "you began to see the police coming in from either Orange County or the state. There were not enough police from the small town of Chapel Hill to keep up with it." Following the incident at the Rock Pile, the Chapel Hill police logged in 400 hours of overtime in three weeks and arrested seventy-five. In another incident at a restaurant outside of town, a waitress straddled one of the demonstrators who was sitting-in and urinated on him. Eighteen demonstrators were arrested.

The sit-ins were, as Jim Wallace recounts, fairly straightforward. "There were two things that always happened. The demonstrators were always singing, whether they were marching or sitting-in. And when they marched, they always carried an American flag. It was kind of interesting that they were not carrying a North Carolina flag; they were carrying the American flag. And this was

[5]Interview with Karen L. Parker, June 21, 2011; diary entry for December 18, 1963 from the Karen L. Parker Diary (#5275-z), Southern Historical Collection, Wilson Library, University of North Carolina at Chapel Hill. The diary can be viewed online at http://www.lib.unc.edu/mss/inv/p/Parker,Karen_L.html.

at a time when the Confederate flag was still being openly and proudly displayed. But the intensity grew, there would be more and more sit-ins, and there would be more and more arrests. There might be a restaurant here or there that integrated but they were few and far between."

Some of the demonstrators opted to be jailed rather than pay fines levied against them. Karen Parker, who was documenting her experiences as a black student on a white campus in her diary, wrote on December 18, 1963: "On Saturday, the 14th, I decided to go to jail. It was no fun at all."[5]

Access Denied—Officially

After many months of discussion and negotiation, a public accommodations ordinance was set to come before the Chapel Hill Board of Aldermen for a vote on Monday January 13, 1964. The solution to the problem seemed to be in sight. On the eve of that vote, a group of 170 met in Durham, heard speeches from CORE's national director, James Farmer, and others, and then marched three hours in the freezing rain from Durham to Chapel Hill. The WALK FOR FREEDOM was staged to support passage of the ordinance. Some of Jim Wallace's most vivid images are of this march.[1]

In addition, a two-page ad was taken out in the Sunday edition of the *Chapel Hill Weekly* that stated, "We, the persons whose names appear below, urge the passage of a public accommodations ordinance in Chapel Hill that will forbid discrimination because of race." It was signed by hundreds of local citizens.

Nevertheless, on Monday night in Chapel Hill Town Hall, the board voted down the bill 4-2. The aldermen suggested that a mediation board be set up to hear individual disputes regarding segregated establishments as a solution. At the time of the defeat, 25 percent of all businesses in Chapel Hill were still segregated.

After this defeat, the focus of the demonstrators turned to February 1, 1964, which was important for two reasons. First, it was the deadline that CORE had given Chapel

[1] *Baltimore Afro-American*, January 14, 1964.

Marchers walk in freezing rain from Durham to Chapel Hill on January 12, 1964, in support of a pending local public accommodations ordinance.

[2]*Wilmington* (NC) *Star-News*, February 2, 1964, 30.

Hill to integrate. If not, James Farmer pledged to marshal his resources on Chapel Hill. Secondly and symbolically, it was the fourth anniversary of that first sit-in in Greensboro. The anniversary was marked with a large-scale demonstration in Chapel Hill during which twenty-three people were arrested.[2]

In preparation for a Freedom March from Durham to Chapel Hill, demonstrators attended a rally at Chapel Hill's First Baptist Church to hear civil rights leader James Farmer speak.

Opposite. Supporters of a Chapel Hill public accommodations ordinance pack the First Baptist Church. The Chapel Hill Freedom Committee organized a thirteen-mile Freedom March on January 12, 1964, from Durham to Chapel Hill to support passage of the pending ordinance.

The Chapel Hill Board of Aldermen, led by Mayor
Sandy McClamrock (in center, with white hair),
debate the proposed public accommodations
ordinance. Despite the march, the vote failed.

Quinton Baker, one of the leaders of the Chapel Hill Freedom Movement, speaks at the First Baptist Church rally for the Durham-Chapel Hill March.

John Dunne, a leader of the Chapel Hill Freedom Movement, addresses the First Baptist Church rally for the Durham-Chapel Hill March.

Durham-Chapel Hill Walk for Freedom.

Mass Protest/
Civil Disobedience/
Human Chains

The following Saturday, February 8, 1964, demonstrators staged a massive protest following the UNC-Wake Forest University basketball game in an attempt to draw national attention to the civil rights struggle in Chapel Hill. Sit-ins blocked the exits to the Woollen Gymnasium parking lots. On the other side of the UNC campus, marches and sit-ins completely blocked Franklin Street. There were also sit-ins on the roads leading to Chapel Hill, stopping all traffic entering or leaving town. There were massive arrests that day. Charges were filed against the demonstrators for blocking traffic and resisting arrest. There would be trials ahead.

Then, beginning on March 23, lasting through Holy Week, and ending on Easter on March 29, as the demonstrators awaited trial, a fast—or what one local paper deemed a "hunger strike"—was staged in front of the Franklin Street post office. Leaflets were distributed to passersby detailing the motivations behind their protest. On the reverse side was a list of all the known segregated businesses remaining in town at the time—twenty-nine in all. By the third day of the fast, John Dunne reported that he and the

Several weeks after the Chapel Hill Board of Aldermen failed to pass a public accommodation ordinance, the Chapel Hill Freedom Movement retaliated with a series of sit-ins and marches. On February 8, 1964, demonstrations like this one on Franklin Street effectively disrupted the town.

[1] *Spartanburg Herald-Journal*, March 25, 1964, 1; *New York Times*, March 28, 1964. The *New York Times* covered the fast and noted that on the last night of the fast, the Ku Klux Klan had planned its first rally in the Chapel Hill area in many years. According to the *Times*, it would include "an auto caravan of robed, but not hooded, Klansmen through Chapel Hill" (25). According to Wallace, fellow *Daily Tar Heel* staffer Mickey Blackwell, and a number of printed sources, there is nothing to suggest that the Klan actually rode through Chapel Hill.

others were feeling "kind of dizzy" on their diet of water and cigarettes. A student who was against the protest put up a sign reading "DON'T FEED THE ANIMALS."[1]

The Holy Week fast was the prelude to the trials of the demonstrators, which were assigned to Judge Raymond Mallard of the Orange County Superior Court. Although the charges against most of those arrested, including Karen Parker, were dropped, he set out to harshly punish their leaders. For starters, Mallard made the accused wait to be tried. As Quinton Baker later recalled, "He would not set a trial date or give us a calendar. He would make us come to court, and we sat there for six weeks from eight in the morning to five in the afternoon. He would not allow us to read, he would not allow us to talk, or anything, we had to sit there in the courtroom and be quiet and listen."

Then in April came a long, publicized trial, during which Mallard decided to strike a heavy blow against the Chapel Hill movement, especially against the student leadership, which he treated more severely than the rest of the local movement. The sentences imposed were severe. *Daily Tar Heel* staffer Mickey Blackwell characterized them as "very unfair." As Wallace recalls, "The judge in Hillsborough just threw the book at them all and called them all Communists and it ended up with most of the leaders going to jail."

Dunne and Cusick received twelve months hard labor with an additional two years in prison to begin at the court's discretion in the next five years. Baker and a student from the class of 1964 named Lou Calhoun were given six months hard labor and ordered to return to court in August for a second sentencing. When Calhoun told the judge he was still obliged to put the command of God before the law, he was given an extra six months.

After the death of John F. Kennedy, the fate of the Civil Rights Act was left in the hands of President Lyndon B. Johnson who, before becoming vice president, had served more than two decades in Congress as a congressman and senator from Texas. He used his connections and the outpouring of emotion after the President's assassination to get the act passed.

On July 2, 1964, President Johnson signed the Civil Rights Act into law after it had been passed by Congress earlier in the day. It was the most sweeping legislation of its kind since Reconstruction, outlawing segregation in businesses such as theaters, restaurants, and hotels. It banned discriminatory practices in employment and ended segregation in public places such as swimming pools, libraries, and public schools. The Civil Rights Act was a crucial step in achieving the movement's initial goal: full legal equality.

Wallace says, "It was at once a triumph for those in the movement in Chapel Hill and a real defeat for local leaders, who felt that all the demonstrations had been for naught. It took intervention by the federal government to finally integrate all the restaurants in Chapel Hill." And even worse, a dozen leaders of the local movement were in prison or working on road gangs at hard labor under the blazing summer sun.

Above. Arthur Beaumont reaches for a demonstrator blocking the entrance to the Woollen Gym parking lot.

Right. The sit-in at the exit of the Woollen Gym parking lot brings cars to a standstill after the end of the UNC-Wake Forest basketball game.

On February 8, 1964, protesters block the drive to
UNC's Woollen Gym, where a basketball game with
Wake Forest was in progress. Arthur Beaumont, chief
of the UNC campus police, is on the left.

Opposite. A woman stares at protesters who block her car from exiting the university parking lot.

Right. Arthur Beaumont drags a sit-in protester away from the entrance to the Woollen Gym parking lot.

Daily Tar Heel staffers Mickey Blackwell and Wayne King, at far right, observe the sit-in that paralyzes Franklin Street on February 8, 1964.

Students and townspeople line the intersection in front of the Chapel Hill Town Hall to watch as arrested demonstrators are brought to the jail.

Protesters plant themselves in a crosswalk on Franklin
Street. One carries a sign that reads, "We reserve the
right to refuse service to Jim Crow."

The Ku Klux Klan Reacts

Just days after passage of the Civil Rights Act of 1964, a segregationist dashed off a derisive postcard to James Farmer of CORE: "Dear Sir—Now that you have a worldwide platform, tell the whites what we really want, the freedom to murder, rape, knife, and pillage. Love, I. M. Black." This was just one example of the anger welling up from the foes of racial integration. The world of white supremacy was crumbling, and it was time for the Ku Klux Klan and its sympathizers to make their presence known—to remind and recruit.

On July 30, 1964, a small item appeared on the front page of the summer edition of *The Tar Heel* under the headline "KKK Plans Open Rally on Saturday."[1] The event was to be staged at 8 p.m. at the intersection of NC Route 86 and Interstate 85 south of Hillsborough near the Dixie Inn, a roadhouse. The announcement noted that local law enforcement would attend the rally to direct traffic and maintain order.

Jim Wallace realized that this was a great opportunity for a photographer. He and *Tar Heel* reporter Mickey Blackwell went together. "When we got to the location of the rally, there were men in uniforms directing the traffic and helping park the cars." Wallace remembers, "But when we got closer we realized that it was Klan security. . . . they were even wearing brown shirts." This was stunning because the Brown Shirts were an early Nazi paramilitary organization in Germany. The two college students parked the car they were using and worked their way into the rally, trying not to attract undue attention.

The burning cross.

[1] Every summer *The Daily Tar Heel* became a weekly known simply as *The Tar Heel*.

"We didn't say much," Wallace recalls. "We just sort of stood on the side and did our thing. They were looking for publicity and they wanted good publicity. They were not overly bright when it comes to trying to figure out what kind of publicity they were going to get. When they wanted to know who we were, we introduced ourselves, and I am not totally convinced to this day that they didn't think I might have been related to the governor of Alabama, (George Wallace). Perhaps that's why I got away with as much as I did."

Through the lens of his Miranda, Wallace watched the Klansmen and women enact their enigmatic rituals. At one point, everyone walked past the leader, who lit their torches with his own. They then formed a circle around the cross and, at the signal, threw their torches toward the gasoline-soaked cross, which burst into flames. The cross was immense, with a telephone pole serving as its vertical element.

"There was a gasoline generator and a guy on the back of a flatbed truck raising hell, ranting and raving about what was happening to America. I remember the speeches from the women. I was surprised to see a woman's auxiliary there. One of the women at the rally stood up and said something like I'd rather see my daughter dead then married to a Negro—although she didn't use the word 'Negro.' Of course, none of them covered their faces, it was our understanding that there was a law that you had to show your face, so you could see the faces of all of them."

As evidenced by the images he captured at the event, Wallace's view of the Klan was unobstructed, but it was not without personal risk, especially for a young photographer making a name for himself locally by chronicling sit-ins and demonstrations. For his part, Blackwell had been writing about the movement in Chapel Hill, so he was in the same boat as Wallace. Mickey Blackwell says that they were just plain scared. "I know

Klansmen line up at the beginning of the
cross-burning ceremony.

photographing the Ku Klux Klan was the only time in any of the things that I ever did—whether it was the March on Washington or whether it was people sitting-in and being arrested, or anything else—where I was concerned for my own safety," says Wallace.

"Concerned" may be an understatement. The Klan had become especially violent at this point in history. On June 21, three civil rights workers had disappeared in Mississippi. Two days after the Klan rally Wallace photographed, the bodies of the three murdered men were found buried in a twenty-three-foot dam. The Klan's involvement was a given. Several days later, on August 8, in Athens, Georgia, four members of the KKK were charged with the murder of Lieutenant Colonel Lemuel Penn, a prominent black educator who had been killed on his way home from an Army Reserve training camp near Washington, D.C. The images of the Klan are among the last Wallace took for the *Tar Heel* and are, perhaps, the most stunning.

Opposite: A Klansman preaches from a platform on the back of a pick-up truck while a cross burns in the background.

p. 96. As the cross-burning ceremony begins, men light their torches and march around the cross.

p. 97. After circling the burning cross, Klansmen throw their torches toward its base.

p. 98. Members of the Klan's women's auxiliary line up next to the men.

p. 99. A Klansman is silhouetted by the burning cross and strewn torches.

The Struggle Continued and Resolved

The events in Chapel Hill made little national news while they were happening and are all but forgotten today. When sociologist David Reisman wrote the introduction to John Ehle's narrative of the Chapel Hill struggle, *The Free Men* (Harper and Row, 1965), he noted that back then, the events in that book were "almost entirely unknown to us." For this reason alone, Jim Wallace's images are important because they reveal a little-known battle in the civil rights struggle. They underscore the point that the overall campaign was larger and ran deeper than is popularly recalled. The images are also sobering in that they depict a local struggle that did not end with a victory, making them all the more poignant.

The university's neutrality did not mean that some of the students who participated did not end up worse off as a result of their activism. John Dunne was a Morehead scholar, an honor named for John Motley Morehead who made his money at Union Carbide. As a result of John Dunne's work with the movement, he lost his scholarship. Wallace explains, "Students who were arrested during the protests never got any support or help from the university."

On December 5, 1964, Governor Terry Sanford commuted the sentences of the Chapel Hill protestors, but as Jim Wallace is quick to point out, Sanford never pardoned those who had been jailed for demonstrating. "I think it is important to note that in

Marchers sing freedom songs to convey their message, elevate their spirits, and boost their courage.

North Carolina Governor Terry Sanford greets black leaders at the conference to discuss the "Negro Protest Movement," on July 3, 1963.

Opposite. Protesters march and sing on Chapel Hill's Franklin Street in front of the post office.

these photographs, everybody you see being arrested still has a criminal record for trespassing, or failure to obey or whatever it was that they were charged with, and some of them were arrested dozens of times." If Wallace paid a price for his remarkable collegiate achievement, it was with truly lousy grades. His official record at the school was less than impressive. His grades were not good and had suffered from his decision to practice journalism rather than study it. It was often hard to find time for classes while working six days a week on *The Daily Tar Heel*. The academic high point of his college years was his first freshman semester, when he achieved a C average, which he did not match again until the day he graduated and needed to get two Bs on his final exams to graduate. "I got a C and an A."

On the other hand, his poor grades meant he was forced to spend a lot of time in summer school, which allowed him to get more images including those of a Fourth of July march and the 1964 Klan rally. Shortly after graduating from UNC in 1964, Wallace was commissioned as an Air Force second lieutenant, and he rolled up the negatives from his Chapel Hill years and packed them away. The irony in this is compelling, because despite Wallace's other accomplishments—and there are many—the pictures he took as a student are his most important legacy. What he created was not just a series of dramatic images, but rather a microcosm of events throughout the country during the most important years of the civil rights era.

The fact that Jim Wallace, rather than a timid and less resourceful individual, was assigned to cover the story of the movement was providential. Wallace himself, and those he depicted in the struggle, showed courage in the moment.

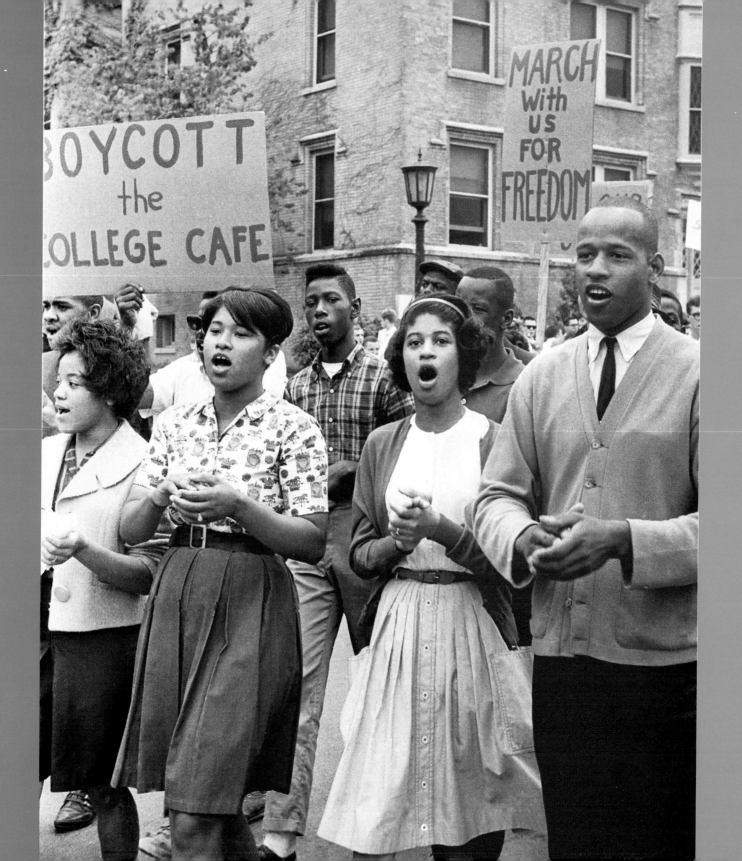

Chronology

May 17, 1954—*Brown v. Board of Education* ruling outlaws segregation in public schools.

September 17, 1955—LeRoy Benjamin Frasier Jr., Ralph Frasier, and John Lewis Brandon become the first black undergraduates to attend UNC-Chapel Hill.

December 1, 1955—Rosa Parks refuses to give up her seat on a Montgomery, Alabama, bus.

February 1, 1960—Four North Carolina Agricultural and Technical State University students sit-in at the Woolworth's lunch counter in Greensboro.

February 28, 1960—Students from Lincoln High School stage the first sit-in in Chapel Hill.

May 4, 1961—Congress of Racial Equality (CORE) sends out Freedom Riders across the South.

June 1, 1963—Governor George Wallace vows to defy an injunction ordering integration of the University of Alabama.

June 11, 1963—Mayor's Committee on Integration recognizes that only an ordinance can force integration in all Chapel Hill businesses.

June 25, 1963—The North Carolina General Assembly passes the "Speaker Ban Law," generally considered a means of thwarting the civil rights marches that were taking place in Raleigh and other places in the state.

July 29, 1963—Thirty-four people are arrested at the Chapel Hill/Carrboro Merchant's Association sit-in.

August 28, 1963—Martin Luther King, Jr., delivers "I Have a Dream" speech at the March on Washington for Jobs and Freedom.

November 22, 1963—President John F. Kennedy is assassinated

December 1, 1963—A protester is doused with ammonia at a sit-in at the Rock Pile. This occurs at the beginning of a three-week span of intense protesting. Chapel Hill police log 400 hours of overtime and arrest seventy-five.

January 13, 1964—The Chapel Hill Board of Aldermen rejects the proposed accommodations ordinance by a 4-2 vote.

January 13, 1964—In response to the rejection of the ordinance, CORE issues an ultimatum that Chapel Hill has until February 1 to integrate fully.

February 8, 1964—Protesters run onto the court during a UNC-Wake Forest basketball game and human chains block cars from leaving parking lots after the game.

March 1964—An eight-day Holy Week fast is staged in front of the Franklin Street post office.

April 1964—217 Demonstrators are brought to trial on nearly 1,500 charges; many begin active prison sentences.

July 2, 1964—President Johnson signs the Civil Rights Act of 1964 into law.

December 5, 1964—Governor Terry Sanford commutes the sentences of the Chapel Hill demonstrators, but does not pardon them.

The Chronology is based on the timeline prepared for the 2009 exhibit *I Raised My Hand to Volunteer*, part of a project that included a physical exhibit mounted in the Manuscripts Department of Wilson Library from January 23, 2007 through June 15, 2007 (http://www.lib.unc.edu/mss/exhibits/protests/timeline.html).

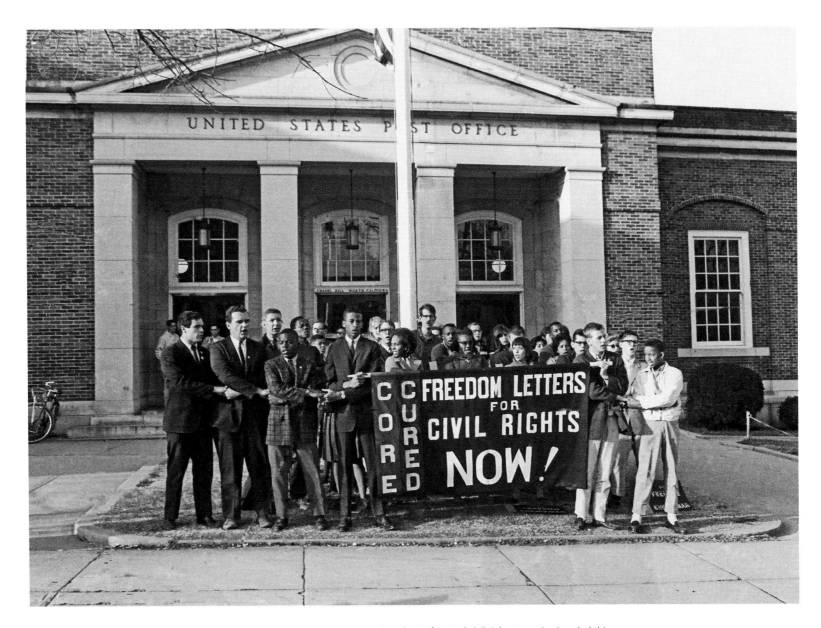

Members of several civil rights organizations led this holiday march on December 7, 1963. Carrying letters addressed to political leaders to urge anti-discrimination legislation, they requested that fellow Chapel Hill citizens follow suit and "Send Freedom Letters for Christmas."

After Chapel Hill

Quinton Baker is the principal consultant with QE Baker Associates, a management consulting service in Hillsborough, North Carolina. His focus is on community-based and community-led organizations, public and private agencies, and institutions that are committed to reaffirming an inclusive participatory democracy.

Dr. Michael C. Blackwell continued in journalism and went into seminary in 1967. He is president of Baptist Children's Homes of North Carolina, based in Thomasville.

Police Chief William D. Blake continued as police chief until the time of his death on September 18, 1978. "He and I exchanged Christmas cards for a number of years until he died a couple of years ago," said Pat Cusick in a 1989 interview. "Very interesting guy."

Patrick Cusick left prison and went back to Boston, where he worked on anti-poverty and community issues. He died in 2004 after a lifetime of fighting diabetes.

John Dunne was released on parole from his North Carolina sentence in the summer of 1964. He moved to Connecticut and, in the fall of that year, returned to school to finish his senior year at Harvard University, where he received a scholarship. In 1972, Dunne graduated from Yale Law School, practiced law briefly in Boston, then moved his practice to Norwich, Vermont, in 1975. Dunne married Faith Weinstein, a professor of Education at Dartmouth College, and had two children, Matthew and Josh. While in Norwich, Dunne was an active supporter of children's theater and Upper Valley Youth Services. Dunne died of cancer on December 26, 1982.

Wayne King worked at *The Detroit Free Press*, where he shared in a Pulitzer Prize for coverage of the 1967 Detroit riots, and *The New York Times*, where he was twice nominated for the Pulitzer before leaving to teach journalism at Wake Forest University. He retired in May 2011.

Karen L. Parker, an activist in the 1963–64 sit-ins, became, in 1965, the first black female to graduate from UNC. After graduating, Parker was a copy editor for the *Grand Rapids Press* in Grand Rapids, Michigan. She also worked for the *Los Angeles Times* and other newspapers before going to work for the *Winston-Salem Journal*. Parker has continued to stay involved with the University of North Carolina, Chapel Hill. She is currently a member of the Board of Directors of the General Alumni Association.

Lindy Pendergrass is Orange County Sheriff, a job he has held since 1982. In early 2011, he helped Wallace identify some of the figures in the photos in this book.

Jim Wallace went into the Air Force after graduating from UNC-Chapel Hill. After his service, he edited a magazine based in Miami. In 1973, he joined the Smithsonian Institution and served as the Director/Curator of the Imaging and Photographic Services. He retired from that job in May 2003.

Notes on the Photographs

The images in this volume were taken decades ago, in the early 1960s. I have identified participants in these photographs through various resources and individuals. While I have attempted to verify names and events whenever possible, any inadvertent errors, misspellings, or omissions are unintentional and solely my own. Additional information about selected images is noted below. —JW

cover—Hilliard Caldwell was later elected to the Board of Aldermen in Carrboro, the town adjoining Chapel Hill.

p. viii-ix—Harold Foster, one of the movement's leaders, and John Farrington are seen at the front of the march.

p. x—In this image, *Daily Tar Heel* reporter Joel Bulkley (wearing sweater and white shirt collar) stands at front left.

p.2—Marchers include Hilliard Caldwell, Alveta Cotton, Shena Johnson, Junior Hines, Harold Foster, Esther Foster, and Jackie Baldwin.

p. 8—Also pictured are Ruby Farrington and Buddy Bynum.

p.10—Most of the picketing students were members of the Wesley Foundation. A Wesley Foundation is a United Methodist campus ministry sponsored in full or in part (depending on the congregation) by the United Methodist Church on a non-church owned and operated campus.

p. 14—Demonstrator Walter Mitchell is seen at center.

p. 17—The leaders in the photos include Hilliard Caldwell, Charlie Foushee, John Fykes, Clementine Farrington, Carl Watson, and Thomas Bynum.

p. 19—Baker is followed by local leaders Harold Foster and Charlie Foushee. William Carter is also pictured .

p. 27—Covering the march, *Daily Tar Heel* reporter Peter Harkness stands at center right.

p. 30—Demonstrators include Renee Booth, Larry Foushee, Wilbert Jones, James Foushee, Raymond Foushee, Evelyn Walker, and Maxine Mason.

p. 31—Student leader John Dunne is seen in the foreground, at the middle right. Bob Brown, a community activist and later the publisher of the independent newsweekly *The North Carolina Anvil,* is at front right. Others include William Riggsbee, William Carter, Demetrins Williams, Christine Page, Clyde Durham, Buddy Bynum, Valerie Farrington, Bernard Farrington, Charles Farrington, Yvonne Jackson, William Fykes, and Ann Lindsey.

p. 39—Among the demonstrators are Quinton Baker, Yvonne Cotton, Rayford Farrington, Calvin Farrington, Paul Farrington, Wayne Page, and Shemone Baldwin.

p. 41—Demonstrators in this image include leaders Pat Cusick and Hilliard Caldwell.

p. 44—Police Chief William Blake stands at far left with his back to the camera.

Sources

p. 72—James Farmer vowed to "close the town down" if the Board of Aldermen failed to pass the pending public accommodations ordinance. Seated behind Farmer are John Knowles, author of *A Separate Peace*, and church pastor Dr. J. R. Manley.

p. 100—Here, Carol Brown Purefoy, Calvin Farrington, Emogene Davis, and Maxine Mason sing during a nighttime demonstration outside a segregated establishment.

p. 103—Marchers include Carol Purefoy, Enda Walker, Patricia Atwater, Hilliard Caldwell, Pete Parrish, and Charlie Warren Foushee.

p. 104—Pictured are Otto White, Ophelia Johnson, Kenny Farrington, Carolyn Farrington, Cynthia Hines, and Johnny Robinson.

p. 106—The front row includes John Dunne, Pat Cusick, Peter Leak, Charlese Cotton, Eugene Riggsbee, and Herman Foushee.

Quinton E. Baker, February 23, 2002. Interview K-0838. Southern Oral History Program Collection (#4007) in the Southern Oral History Program Collection, Southern Historical Collection, Wilson Library, University of North Carolina, Chapel Hill.

Cusick, Pat, June 19, 1989. Interview L-0043. Southern Oral History Program Collection (#4007) in the Southern Oral History Program Collection, Southern Historical Collection, Wilson Library, University of North Carolina, Chapel Hill.

Ehle, John. *The Free Men*. New York: Harper & Row, 1965. (Winston-Salem publisher Press 53 published a revised edition in February, 2007, with updated material.)

Graham, Nicholas. "April 1947: Freedom Ride." This Month in North Carolina History, April 2005. North Carolina Digital History (http://www.learnnc.org/lp/editions/nchist-postwar/6007).

Peck, Jim. "The First Freedom Ride, 1947." *Southern Exposure*, 9, no. 1 (Spring 1981): 36–37.

Following page. Two marchers cool off at the Reflecting Pool on Washington's National Mall.